Speak Street

SUPPORTED BY Mishcon de Reya

This book is designed to help learners improve their English as they explore the history of the streets of London. Speak Street is a not for profit organisation founded as a positive response to negativity towards newcomers. We help people improve their skills and confidence through fun social learning.
This book was created with the support of Mishcon de Reya volunteers. A big thank you to everyone involved.

www.speak-street.com
ISBN 978-1-7394641-1-0
All rights reserved.
No reproduction of any part of this publication by any means is allowed without the prior written permission of the copyright owner.
© Speak Street 2025

Contents

Roman London	4
Medieval London	12
Legal London	20
Women in the City of London	28
The Great Fire of London	36

Speak Street students and volunteers during a visit to Middle Temple Church

Roman London

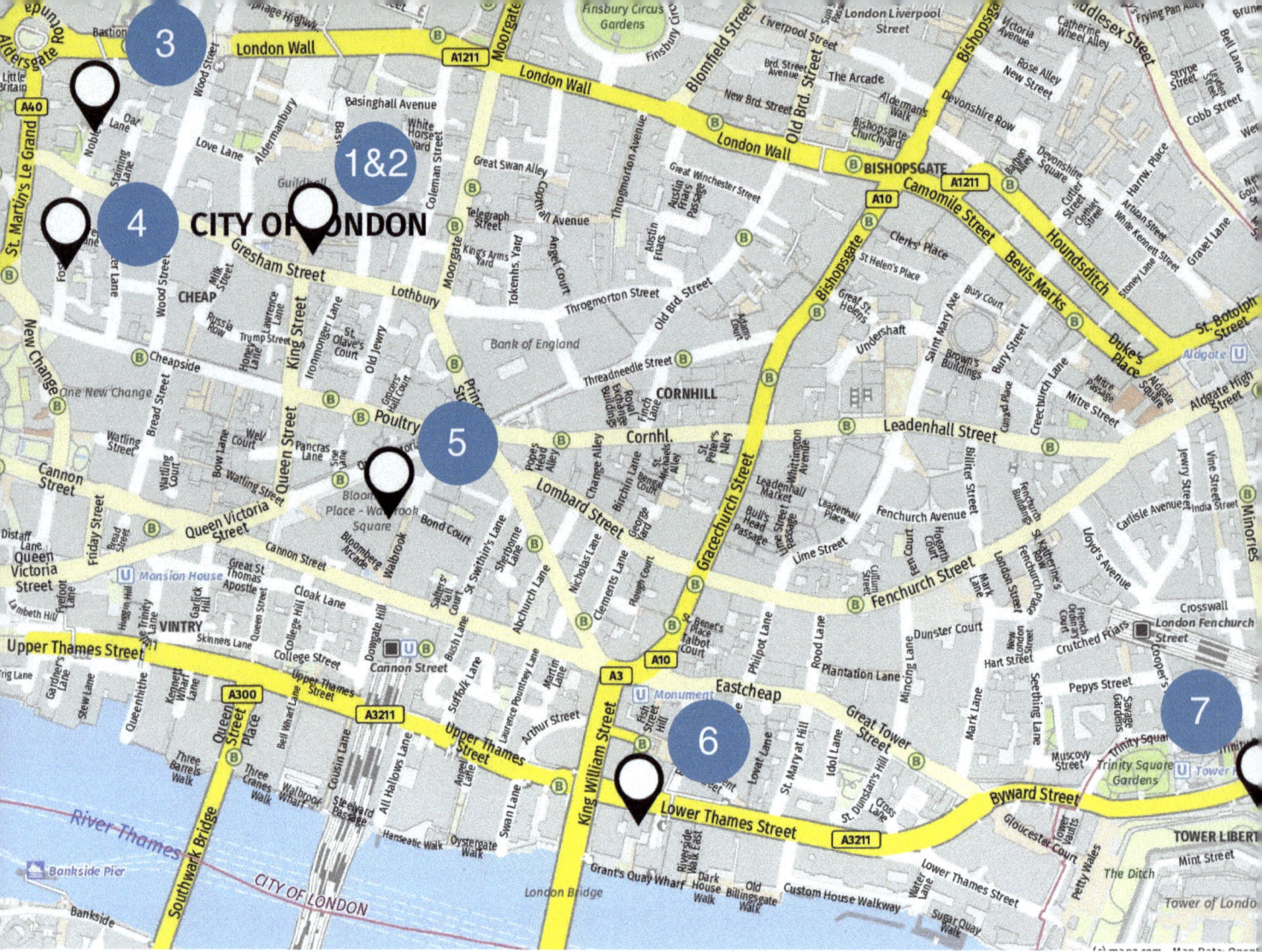

Stop 1: Guildhall Yard

Stop 2: Inside the Roman Amphitheatre remains on Floor A of the Guildhall Art Gallery

Stop 3: Noble Street

Stop 4: St Vedast-Alias Foster Churchyard

Stop 5: Temple of Mithras

Stop 6: St Magnus the Martyr

Stop 7: Roman Wall and Statue of Emperor Trajan

Guildhall Yard

Stop 1 - Guidhall Yard

Can you see the large black circular line that runs around the edge of the yard? That is the outline of the Roman Amphitheatre that was built around 70 CE. This was a huge place where people came to watch entertainment such as gladiator games and animal fights.

Directions: Go inside the Guildhall Art gallery to learn more!

Stop 2 - Inside the Roman Amphitheatre remains on Floor A of the Guildhall Art Gallery

Here we can see the remains of the stone walls and wooden drains. Look closely and you can see two grooves in the wall that maybe was a kind of trap door to release animals out into the arena.

Directions: Turn right out of Guildhall Yard on Gresham Street. Turn right up Noble Street and walk to the end of the road.

Inside the Roman Amphitheatre on floor A of the Guildhall Art Gallery

Stop 3 - Noble Street
Look down and you can see the remains of a Roman Fort. The Romans built a large wall around the city of London. It was possible for around 1000 soldiers to live here. You can see nearby, tall blocks of flats called The Barbican. This is a word that means a walled gate or tower. The Romans brought a type of stone called Ragstone from Kent as London has no natural stones for building.

Directions: Turn around and walk back down Noble Street. Cross Gresham Street and walk down Foster Lane to the end of the road.

Noble Street

St Vedast-Alias Foster Churchyard

Stop 4 - St Vedast-Alias Foster Churchyard
Go up the stairs into the courtyard through the blue door. Can you find an old piece of Roman pavement on the wall? If you look further down the wall you will find an even older brick from Ancient Assyria that's around 3000 years old! It has an ancient type of writing on it and it was brought here by an archeologist called Sir Max Mallowan, who was married to Agatha Christie, a famous British writer.

Directions: Walk left down Cheapside towards Bank junction. Turn down Walbrook at the Magistrates Court and walk down to the Bloomberg Building.

Roman London

Temple of Mithras

Stop 5 - Temple of Mithras
A temple to the Roman god Mithras was found here on the banks of the River Walbrook. The river now flows underneath the pavement. You can visit the temple for free although you might need to book a ticket in advance. Archeologists found lots of interesting things here including sandals, jewellery and writing tablets. We can even read messages that the Romans wrote to each other. In 57 CE the first person uses Londinium (the Roman word for London) as their address. Think how many of us use it as our address today!

Directions: Walk down Walbrook and turn left onto Cannon Street Cross over the large road leading to London Bridge past Monument and turn right into Fish Hill. Walk down Fish Hill and cross Lower Thames Street.

Stop 6 - St Magnus the Martyr You've just walked down Fish Street, one of the original Roman streets leading to the River. The Romans chose this spot to make the first London Bridge across to the otherside. The Thames was much wider then. Look in the porch of St Magnus the Martyr church. Can you find an original piece of Roman wharf? This is where people got off their boats when they arrived in the city. **Directions:** Cross Lower Thames Street and turn right and walk along until St Mary-at-Hill and walk up St Mary-at-Hill. Turn right on East Cheap. Keep walking towards Tower Hill Tube station through Trinity Gardens.

St Magnus the Martyr

Stop 7 - Roman Wall and Statue of Emperor Trajan

You've reached the western edge of the Roman City You can see the wall is much taller here. Can you see the line of red tiles that the Romans included in their walls? Find the statue of the Roman Emperor Trajan. He was in charge when some of the wall was built. The Roman period ended in Britain in 410 CE after the Roman army left after over 350 years. They founded London as a trading city. People lived and worked here from all over the world just as they do today!

Roman Wall and Statue of Emperor Trajan

Roman London

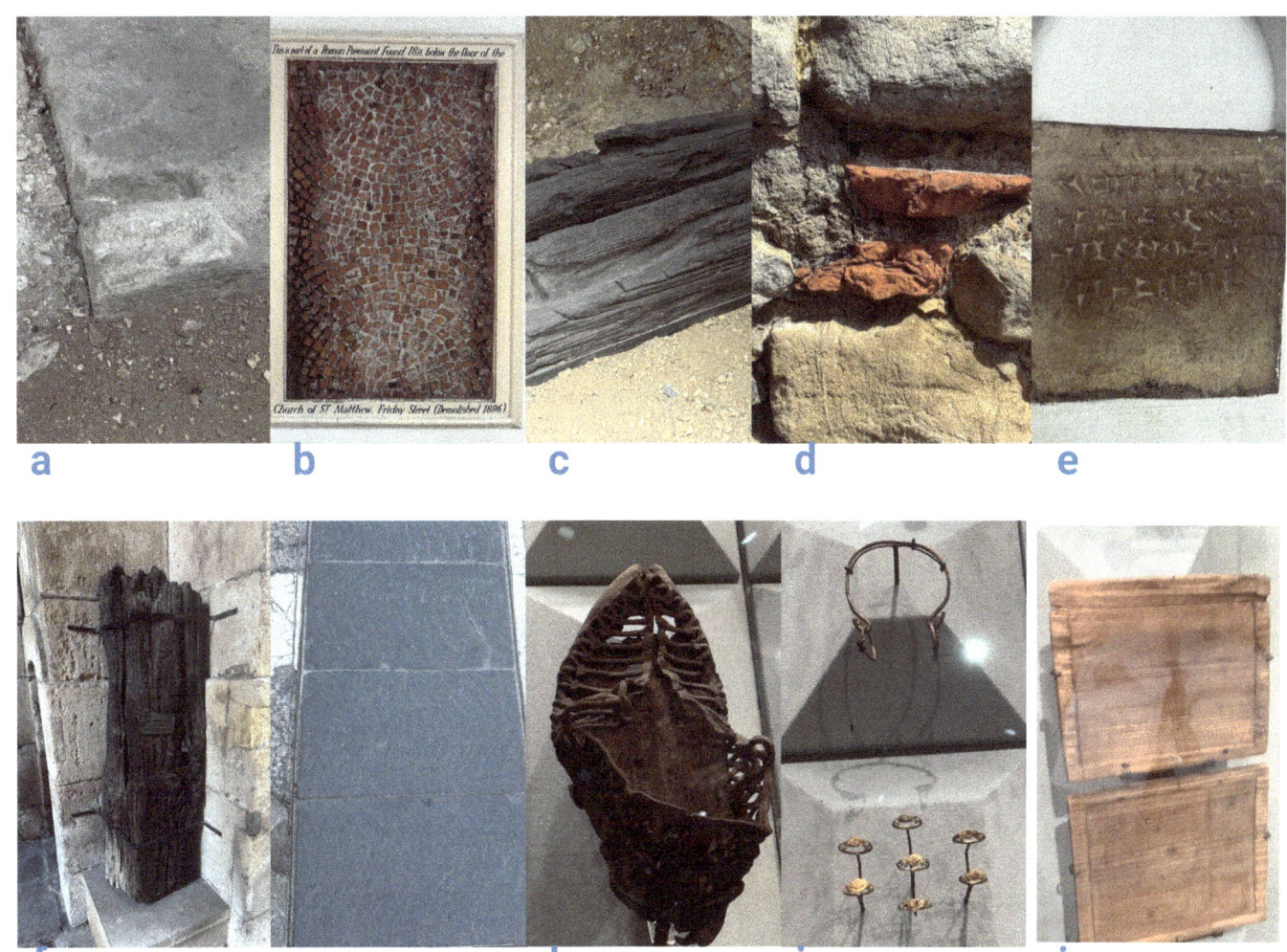

Find these details on the walk.
Match the word to the picture

1. Black floor tiles — Answer
2. Wooden drains — Answer
3. Grooves — Answer
4. Roman Wharf — Answer
5. Red tiles — Answer
6. Sandals — Answer
7. Jewellery — Answer
8. Writing tablets — Answer
9. Roman pavement — Answer
10. Asyrian brick with cuniform writing — Answer

Roman London

Match the following words to describe a Roman Soldier

1. Helmet

2. Sword

3. Shield

4. Armour

5. Belt

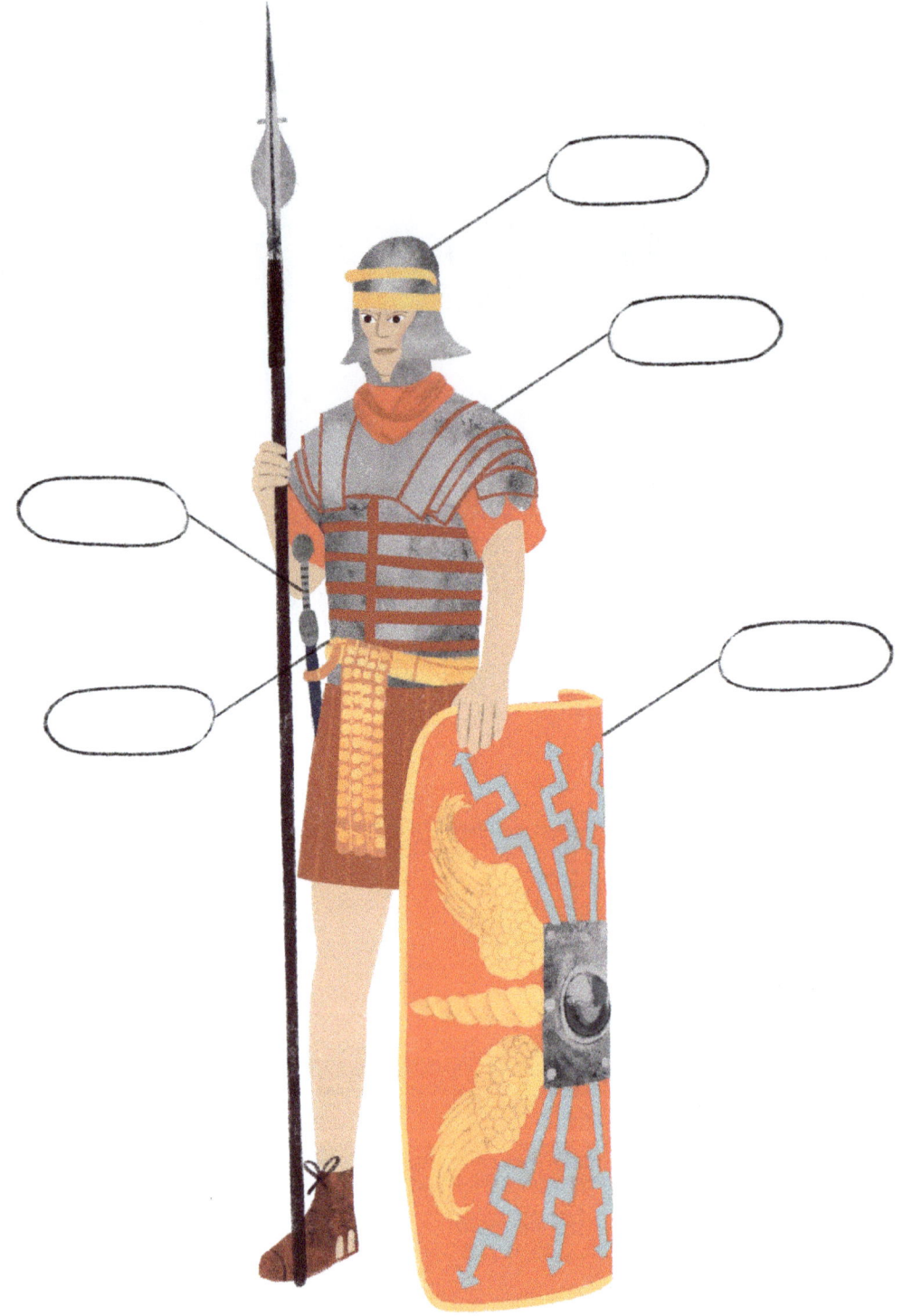

What have you learned about Roman London?

_____

_____

_____

Roman London

Medieval London 500–1500 CE

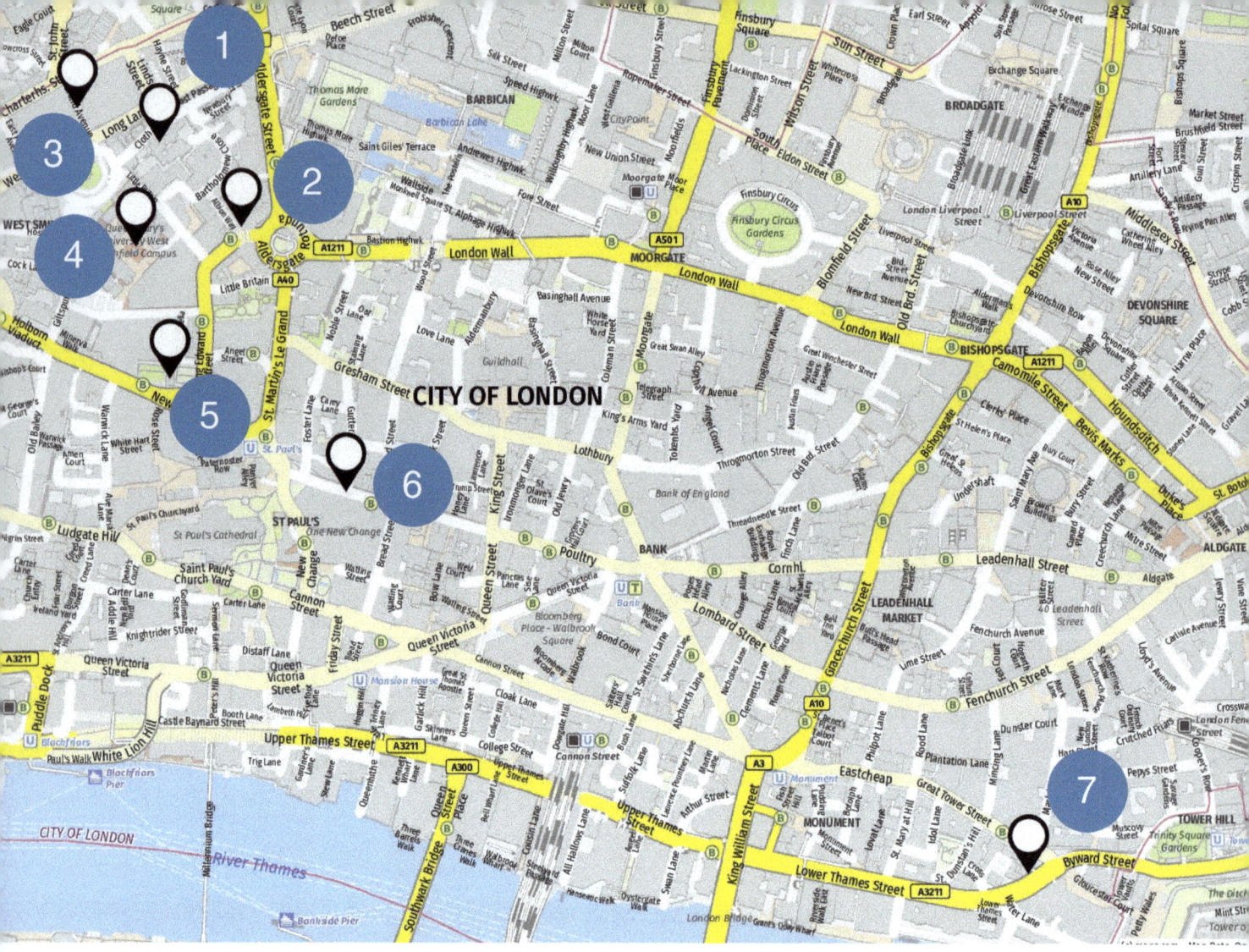

Stop 1: St Bartholomew the Great

Stop 2: William Wallace Memorial

Stop 3: Smithfield Market

Stop 4: St Bartholomew's Hospital

Stop 5: Christchurch Greyfriar

Stop: Cheapside

Stop 7: All Hallows by the Tower

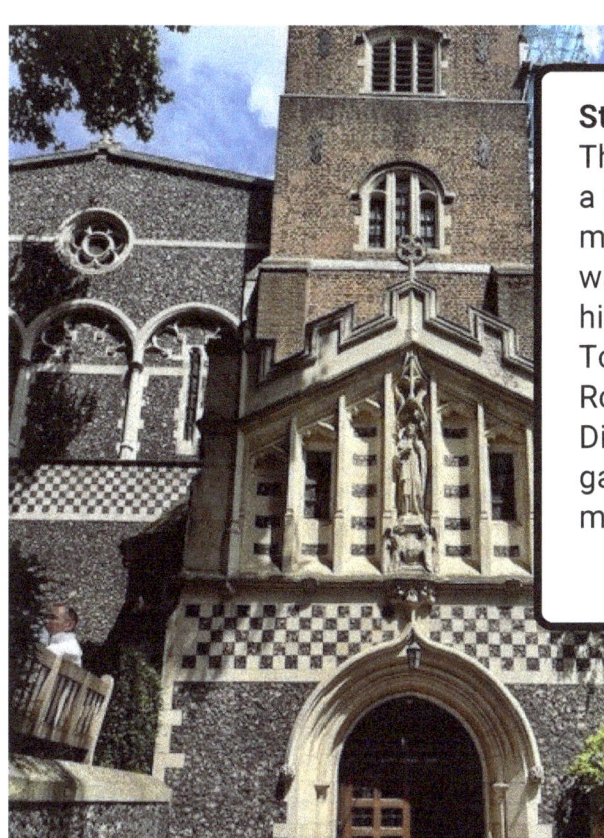
St Bartholomew the Great

Stop 1. St Bartholomew the Great
The Church was built in 1123 CE as a priory. This was a place where monks or friars lived: men who didn't marry and dedicated their life to religion. The founder was a man named Rahere. You can see a carving of him above the door and his tomb is inside the church. Today many films are filmed in the church including Robin Hood Prince of Thieves.
Directions: Walk out under the black and white gatehouse and walk straight ahead to the second memorial on the wall on the left.

William Wallace Memorial

Stop 2. William Wallace Memorial
This is a memorial for William Wallace who was a Scottish Knight who fought against the English in 1297 when the two countries were not joined in the United Kingdom. Wallace was captured by the English King Edward I and executed here in 1305. To many Scottish people, he is a hero so you might see flowers or scottish flags here. In 1995 the actor Mel Gibson played him in the film Braveheart.
Directions: Turn around from Smithfield and follow the wall until you find a gateway with King Henry the VIII standing on top of it.

Medieval London 500-1500 CE

Smithfield Market

Stop 3. Smithfield Market
Smithfield has been a meat market since medieval times. You can see it's colourful iron girders holding up the roof. It was also a popular place for people on horses to joust, where they tried to knock each other of the horse with a long stick. People used to hold the St Bartholomew cloth fair here, where people would sell cloth as well as enjoying food, music and different kind of entertainment. There was even a blindfolded pig who could supposedly tell the time.

Directions: Follow the road around the hospsital and walk down West Smithfield past the red telephone box. Turn left onto Newgate street and keep walking until you reach the next stop

Stop 4. St Bartholomew's Hospital
The hospital has been running for over 900 years. It used to be part of St Bartholomew's church, however from 1534 King Henry VIII broke away from the Catholic church. He also closed the monasteries and took their buildings and money away. Thankfully for Londoners this hospital continued and that's why you can see a statue of the King near the entrance of the hospital.

Directions: Follow the road around the hospital and walk down West Smithfield past the red telephone box. Turn left onto Newgate Street and keep walking until you reach the next stop.

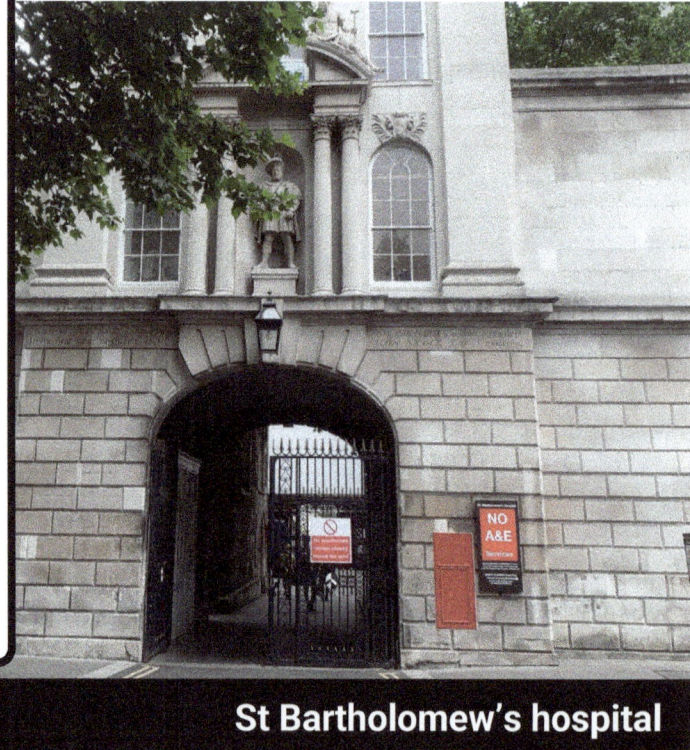
St Bartholomew's hospital

Medieval London 500-1500 CE

Christchurch Greyfriars

Stop 5. Christchurch Greyfriars

Before King Henry VIII closed the monasteries, this used to be the home of the greyfriars, who were similar to monks living in a religious community. There are three medieval queens buried here. Marguerite of France, the second wife of King Edward I as well as Isabella, widow of Edward II, Queen of Scotland. The heart of Eleanor of Provence, wife of Henry III, is also buried here. The church used to also be a school which still exists today but it moved to South London. The church was bombed in the Second World War and was left as a garden after the war.

Directions: Cross the King Edward Street at the crossing and continue left along Newgate street until you reach Cheapside.

Christchurch Greyfriars

Christchurch Greyfriars

Medieval London 500-1500 CE

Cheapside

Stop 6. Cheapside Cheapside is an old English word for Market. This was one of the biggest markets in Europe. The word 'chaps' meaning 'men' might come from the men working on Cheapside. All the streets around Cheapside show what used to be sold in medieval times in them: such as Poultry, Milk Street and Honey Lane. See how many you can spot as you walk down Cheapside. This area of the city was destroyed in the Great Fire of London in 1666. Directions: Walk all the way along Cheapside to Bank Junction. Turn into Lombard Street and then go south into King William Street. Cross Gracechurch street and walk down Eastcheap. Cross Byward Street at the crossing and arrive at All Hallows by the Tower.

All Hallows by the Tower

Stop 7. All Hallows by the Tower
This church was founded in 675 CE by a woman called Ethelburga. The walls of the church are medieval and there are some brass engravings near the altar inside, that date from that time. Inside the church there is an arch by the door that was built in the Saxon period. There is also a beautiful wooden font cover, where babies are baptised, by a wood carver called Grinling Gibbons. The 6th American President, John Quincy Adams, was married at the church. The church is often open and there's lots of interesting things to see including a small museum in the crypt below the church.

Medieval London 500-1500 CE

Find these details on the walk.
Match the word to the picture

1. Tomb   Answer [   ]

2. Carving   Answer [   ]

3. Scottish flag   Answer [   ]

4. Iron girders   Answer [   ]

5. Statue of King Henry VIII   Answer [   ]

6. Brass engravings   Answer [   ]

7. Crypt   Answer [   ]

8. Altar   Answer [   ]

9. Arch   Answer [   ]

10. Garden   Answer [   ]

Match the following words to describe medieval street trader

1. Hood

2. Hose

3. Tunic

4. Boots

5. Cloak

What have you learned about Medieval London?

_____

_____

_____

Medieval London 500-1500 CE

Legal London

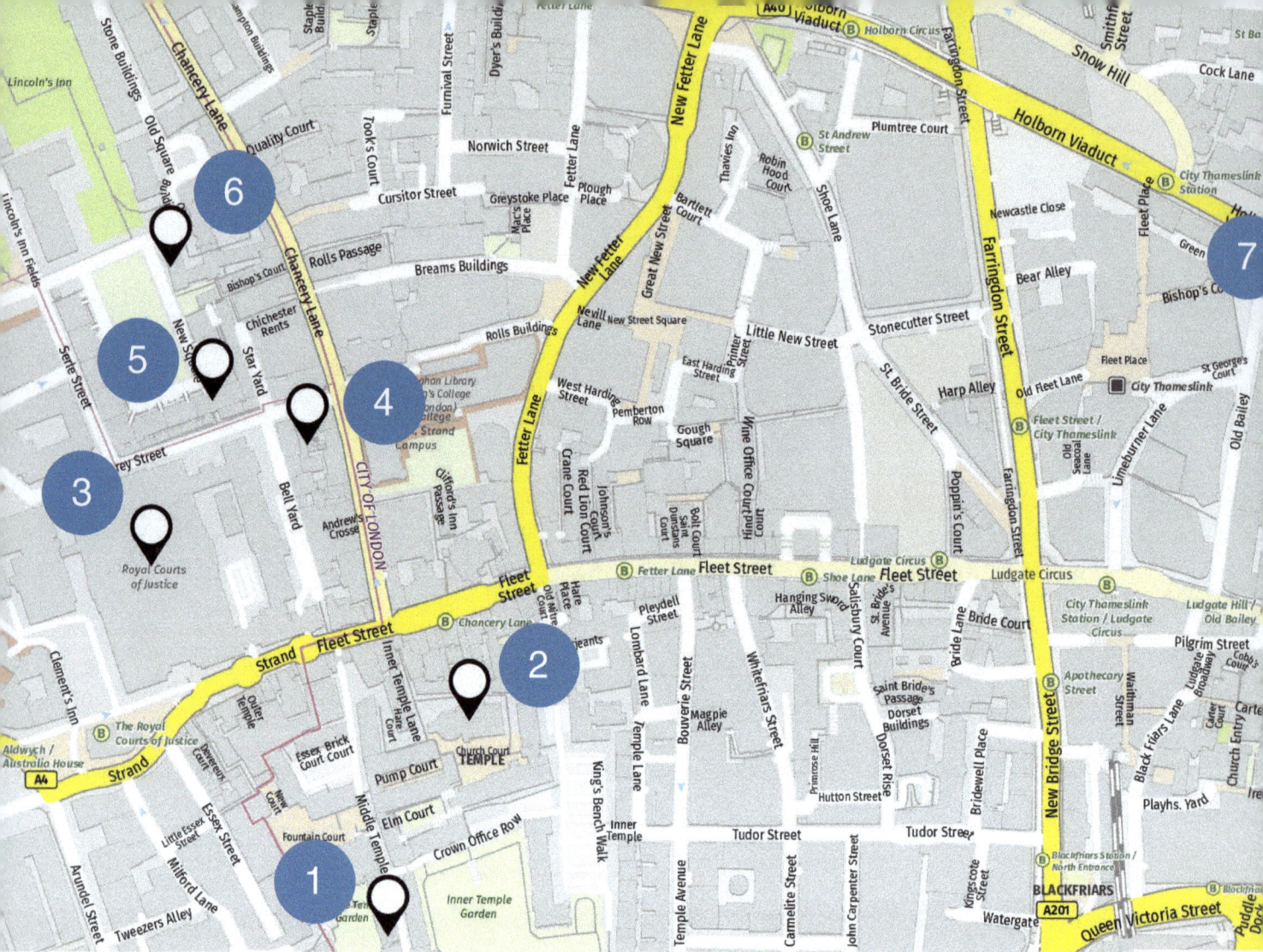

Stop 1: Middle Temple Lane Archway

Stop 2: Temple Church

Stop 3: Royal Courts of Justice

Stop 4: The Law Society's Hall

Stop 5: Wildy and Sons Ltd Booksellers

Stop 6: The Honorable Society of Lincolns Inn

Stop 7: The Old Bailey (Central Criminal Court)

Stop 1. Middle Temple Lane Archway
This area is know as Temple, named after a medieval group of soldier monks, the Knights Templar. This was the location of the Templars headquarters from around 1160. Now Middle Temple and Inner Temple are two of the four Inns of Courts. In order to become a Barrister you must be a member of one of the Inns which are all in London. Can you see the two cherubs on the arch and can you find two lions? Over 400 years ago, Shakespeare's play Twelfth Night was performed here in Middle Temple hall for the first time. A young Indian lawyer called Mahatma Gandhi became a member of Inner temple in 1891. He was later know as Mahatma Gandhi when he led a non-violent independence movement in India against the British Empire. He was disbarred from Inner Temple in 1922 when he was charged with sedition, encouraging people to rebel against British Colonial power. He was readmitted to Inner Temple in 1988 after his death as a mark of great honor. India became independent in 1947.
Directions: Walk through the archway, up Middle Temple Lane, turn right through the tunnel opposite the white arches on the corner of Brick Court.

Middle Temple Lane Archway

Stop 2. Temple Church
The round church was first built and used by the Knights Templar in they 12th Century. They wanted it to look like the Church of the Holy Sepulchre in Jerusalem. The round part of the church is the nave and the rectangle part is the chancel. Can you find a statue of the Knights Templar on a horse holding a shield?
Directions: Turn around, back through the tunnel, then north up Middle Temple Lane until you hit Fleet Street.

Temple Church

Royal Courts of Justice

Stop 3. Royal Courts of Justice The architecture style is gothic revival and it was opened in 1882 by Queen Victoria. The Royal Courts of Justice are where the High Court of England and Wales are. They are the highest court in the country except for the Supreme Court. There is a large, rose shaped window above the entrance. Can you see statues of Jesus, King Solomon and King Alfred on the pinnacles? If you pass through security you can go inside. There are over 1000 rooms inside 31 of them are courtrooms. It is so big one person was found living in the basement for a long time before anyone noticed.
Directions: Turn left out of the main entrance of the Royal Courts of Justice, walk along the Strand and take the first left up Chancery Lane to No. 113.

Stop 4. The Law Society's Hall
The Law Society was founded in the 1820's. There are 4 doric columns at the entrance as well as the Law Society's coat of arms. Can you see the golden lions on the railings? Inside there is a large legal library. The organisation supports solicitors. Its mission is to protect everyone's right to have access to justice in England and Wales. In 1919 women were allowed to sit the Law Society exam for the first time to become a solicitor. Mary Sykes was one of the first women to be allowed to become a solicitor and register with the Law Society in 1919. She also became the first female Mayor of Huddersfield.
Directions: Continue walking north up Chancery Lane, take the first left onto Carey Street, then turn right into the alleyway at the signpost for Wildy & Sons.

The Law Society's hall

Legal London

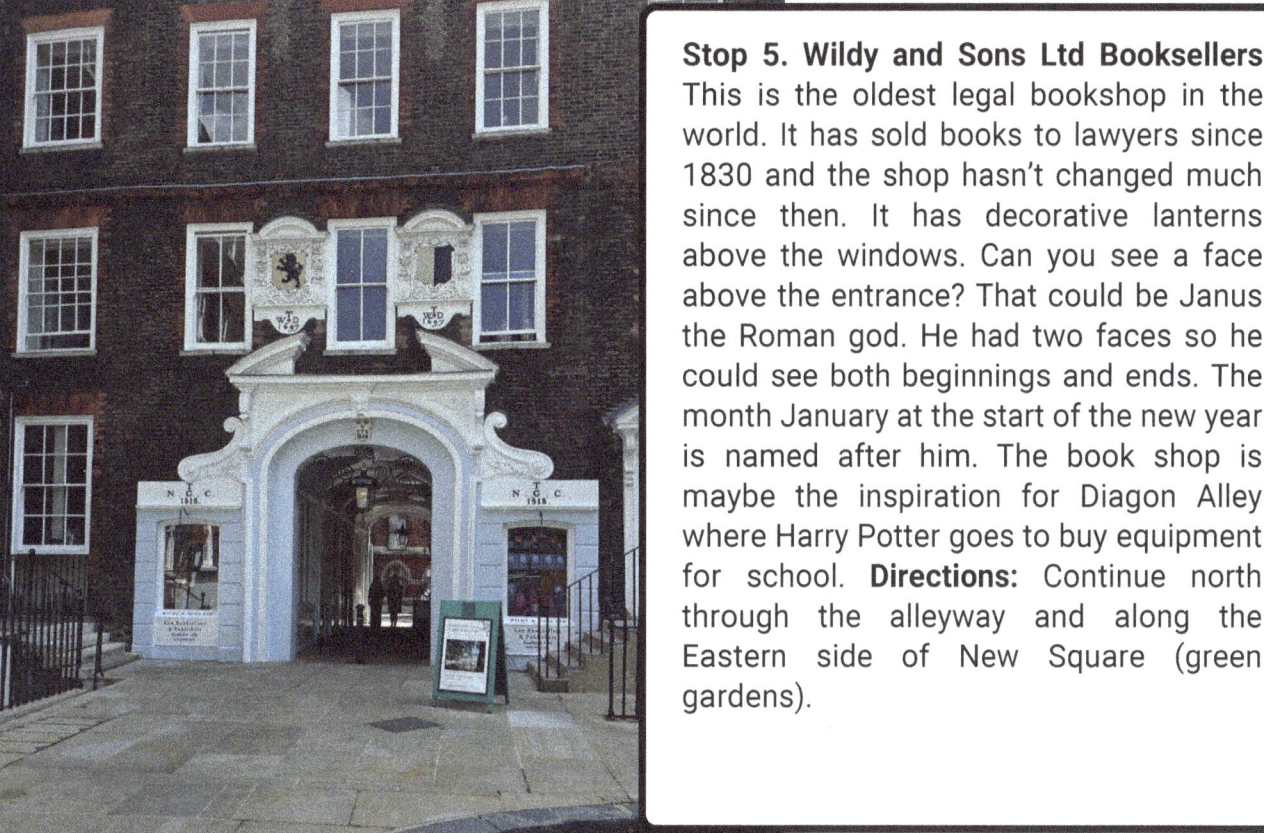
Wildy and Sons Ltd Booksellers

Stop 5. Wildy and Sons Ltd Booksellers
This is the oldest legal bookshop in the world. It has sold books to lawyers since 1830 and the shop hasn't changed much since then. It has decorative lanterns above the windows. Can you see a face above the entrance? That could be Janus the Roman god. He had two faces so he could see both beginnings and ends. The month January at the start of the new year is named after him. The book shop is maybe the inspiration for Diagon Alley where Harry Potter goes to buy equipment for school. **Directions:** Continue north through the alleyway and along the Eastern side of New Square (green gardens).

The honorable Society of Lincolns Inn

Stop 6. The Honorable Society of Lincolns Inn
This is one of the Inns of Courts. The oldest building The Old Hall was built in 1490. Five former Prime Ministers have been members here, including Presidents of Pakistan, Malaysia, Israel and Trinidad and Tobago. The gardens are open to the public during the week. The symbol of the Inn is the purple lion, can you find one?
Directions: Exit right onto Chancery Lane, then turn left/north until you reach Holborn, then turn right and continue walking for circa 15 mins along Holborn viaduct and turn right at Old Bailey.

Stop 7 - The Old Bailey (Central Criminal Court) The Old Bailey is where major criminal trials happen. It has 4 courts and 90 cells. The building was built in 1902, it says, above the entrance, punish the wrong dooers and protect the children of the poor. Can you see stone statues of a recording angel between figures representing fortitude and truth? There have been many famous trials here over the years, including the writer Oscar Wilde, who was gay and prosecuted for indecency in 1895. Suffragettes, women fighting for the right to vote, were also prosecuted here for damaging property as a protest. Thanks to the campaigning of earlier generations, both women and LGBT rights are protected in law today.

The Old Bailey (Central Criminal Court)

Find these details on the walk.
Match the word to the picture

1. Recording Angel   Answer
2. Shield   Answer
3. Lantern   Answer
4. Railings   Answer
5. Pinnacle   Answer
6. Nave   Answer
7. Chancel   Answer
8. Cherub   Answer
9. Knight   Answer
10. Ionic Column   Answer

Match the following words to describe Helena Normanton one of the first Female Barrister

1. Collarette

2. Gown

3. Barristers wig

4. Brief case

5. Legal dictionary

What have you learned about Legal London?
_____
_____
_____
_____

Women in the City of London

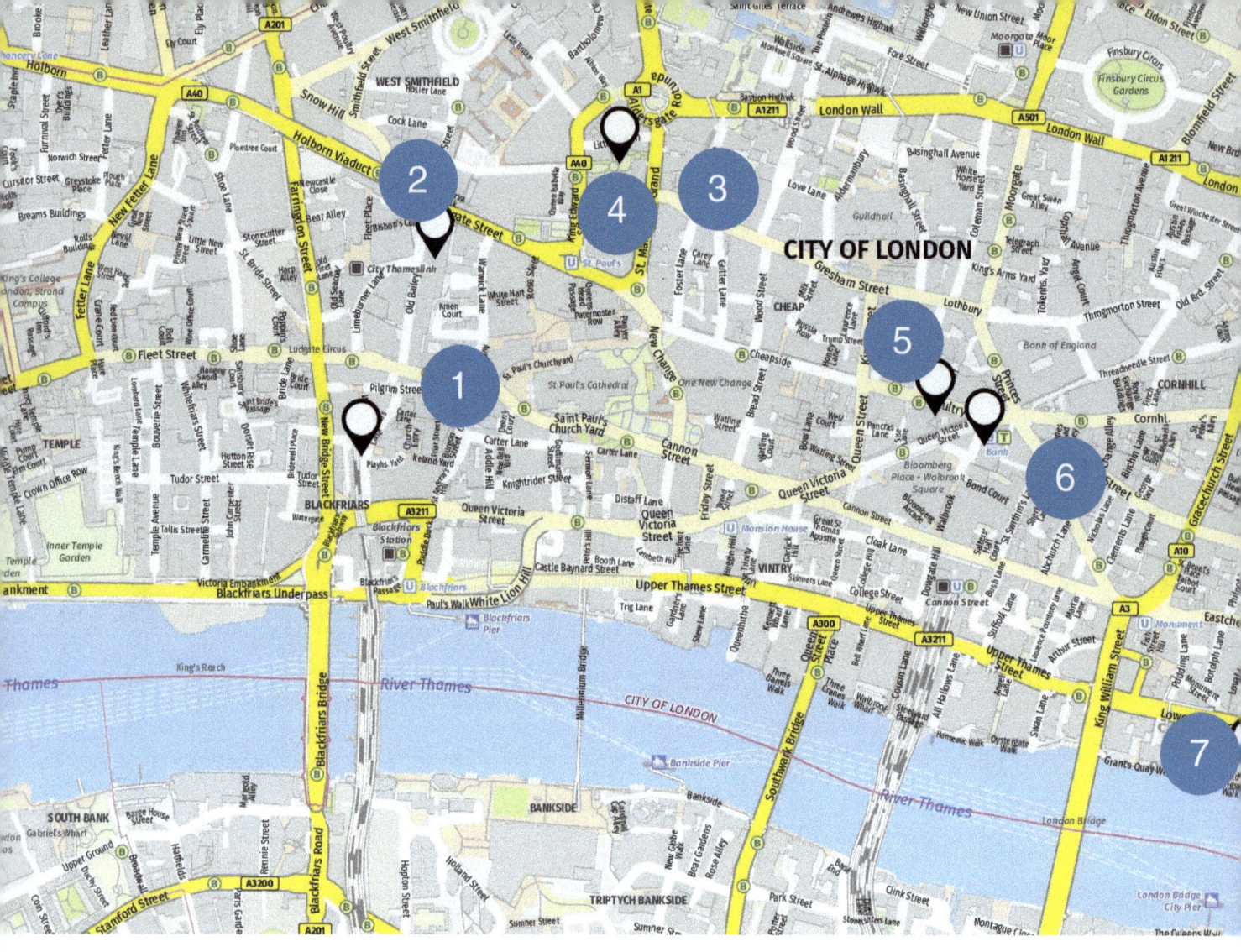

Stop 1: Apothecaries Hall

Stop 2: The Old Bailey (Central Criminal Court)

Stop 3: Postman's Park

Stop 4: Temple Bar

Stop 5: No 1. Poultry

Stop 6: Mansion House

Stop 7: Old Billingsgate Fishmarket

Apothecaries Hall

Stop 1 - Apothecaries Hall

The Apothecaries society is a livery company. This is a kind of trade organisation which dates back to 1180 CE. The livery hall is the oldest in London. 'Apothecary' is an old word for pharmacist. Many pharmacists have taken their exams here including Elizabeth Garrett Anderson in 1865. She was the first ever qualified female doctor in the UK. Each livery company has their own coat of arms or badge. Can you see the unicorns and greek god, Apollo, fighting a dragon?

Directions: Cross Ludgate Hill and walk down Old Bailey.

Stop 2 - The Old Bailey (Central Criminal Court)

The Old Bailey is the Central Criminal Court, however, until 1904 it was the site of the infamous Newgate Prison. The prison was very smelly and dirty. In 1813, Elizabeth Fry visited the prison and campaigned for better treatment of prisoners, especially female prisoners and their children who were sometimes inprisoned with their mothers. There is a statue of Elizabeth Fry inside the building. Look out for golden statue of Lady Justice on top of the dome. She is carrying a sword and scales of justice.

Directions: Walk north on Old Bailey and turn into Newgate Street.

The Old Bailey

Postmans Park

Stop 3 - Postman's Park
This park opened in 1880 on the site of three former churchyards. The artist George Frederick Watts created a memorial to people who died trying to save someone else. Look at the memorial. There is one plaque to Alice Ayers. She was a young nanny who saved 3 children from a fire but then died falling from a window. In 2004, the main character in a film called Closer is walking through the park and chooses the name Alice Ayers as a new name for herself after seeing the memorial.
Directions: Walk south of King Edward Street, cross the road and walk down Newgate Street to Paternoster Square.

Stop 4 - Temple Bar Temple Bar is a stone archway built by Christopher Wren. It used to be in a different location at the entrance to the city. Can you spot statues of kings James I, Charles I, Charles II, and Queen Anne of Denmark on it? They used to put the heads of executed traitors on spikes on it. In 1880, a banjo-playing barmaid called Valerie Meux convinced her husband to buy Temple Bar. They moved Temple Bar to their house outside London. She used to have parties in the little room in the arch. In 2004, Temple Bar was renovated and moved back to Paternoster Square. **Directions:** Walk down Cheapside, continue on Poultry.

Temple Bar

Women in London

Stop 5 - No 1. Poultry

The building here today was built in 1997. When they were building it, they found an old Roman street underneath. There was also a layer of burnt soil from around 61 CE. This is when Queen Bouddica led a rebellion against the Romans. She and her army burned the Roman city of London to the ground because she didn't want the Romans to take over control of her land. Many people think she was a brave warrior queen, a symbol of the fight for freedom and justice.

Directions: Walk back to Bank station until you reach Mansion House.

No. 1 Poultry

Stop 6 - Mansion House

Mansion House was built in 1752 as the home of the Lord Mayor of London. This mayor is for the small area called the city of London which is different from the Mayor of London who is responsible for the whole of London. Can you see the Corinthian columns at the entrance? There were also cells for criminals in the cellars including one for women called the "birdcage". In 1912, 4 suffragettes fighting for Women's rights to vote, smashed the windows of Mansion House. They were imprisoned in the cells and sent to Holloway Prison Women gained the right to vote in 1918.

Directions: Walk down King William Street.

Mansion House

Stop 7 - Old Billingsgate Fishmarket
In 1699, this building close to the Thames, became London's official fishmarket. In 1873 the building we see today was built. Can you see the fish weathervane on top of the building as well as fish in the ironwork? Women who worked in the market were sometimes called 'Fishwives'. They had a reputation for swearing, drinking and sometimes being aggressive. They were independent business women and this made them tough and able to look after themselves in the busy and sometimes violent London streets. Women are not always as visible as men in historical records. Generations of women have fought for greater equality. Historical research helps us to uncover their untold stories.

Old Billingsgate Fishmarket

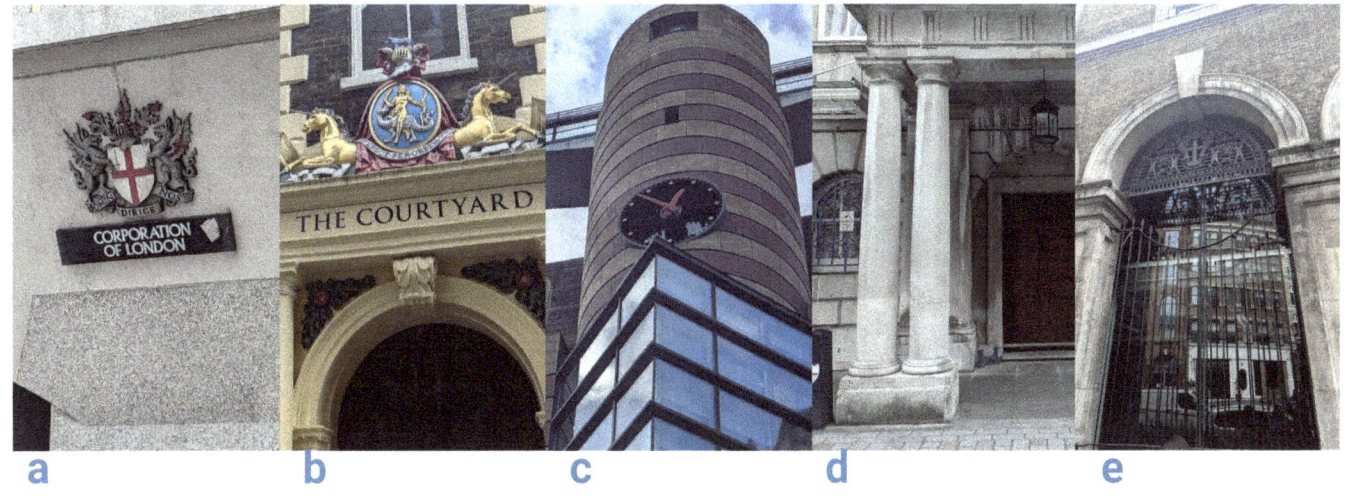

Find these details on the walk.
Match the word to the picture

1. Ironwork   Answer
2. Weathervane   Answer
3. Doric Column   Answer
4. Queen Anne of Denmark   Answer
5. Memorial   Answer
6. Lady Justice   Answer
7. Scales of Justice   Answer
8. Coat of arms   Answer
9. Unicorn   Answer
10. Clock   Answer

Match the following words to describe a Suffragette

1. Blouse

2. Broach

3. Sash

4. Banner

5. Feather

What have you learned about Women from London's history?
_____
_____
_____
_____

Women in London

The Great Fire of London

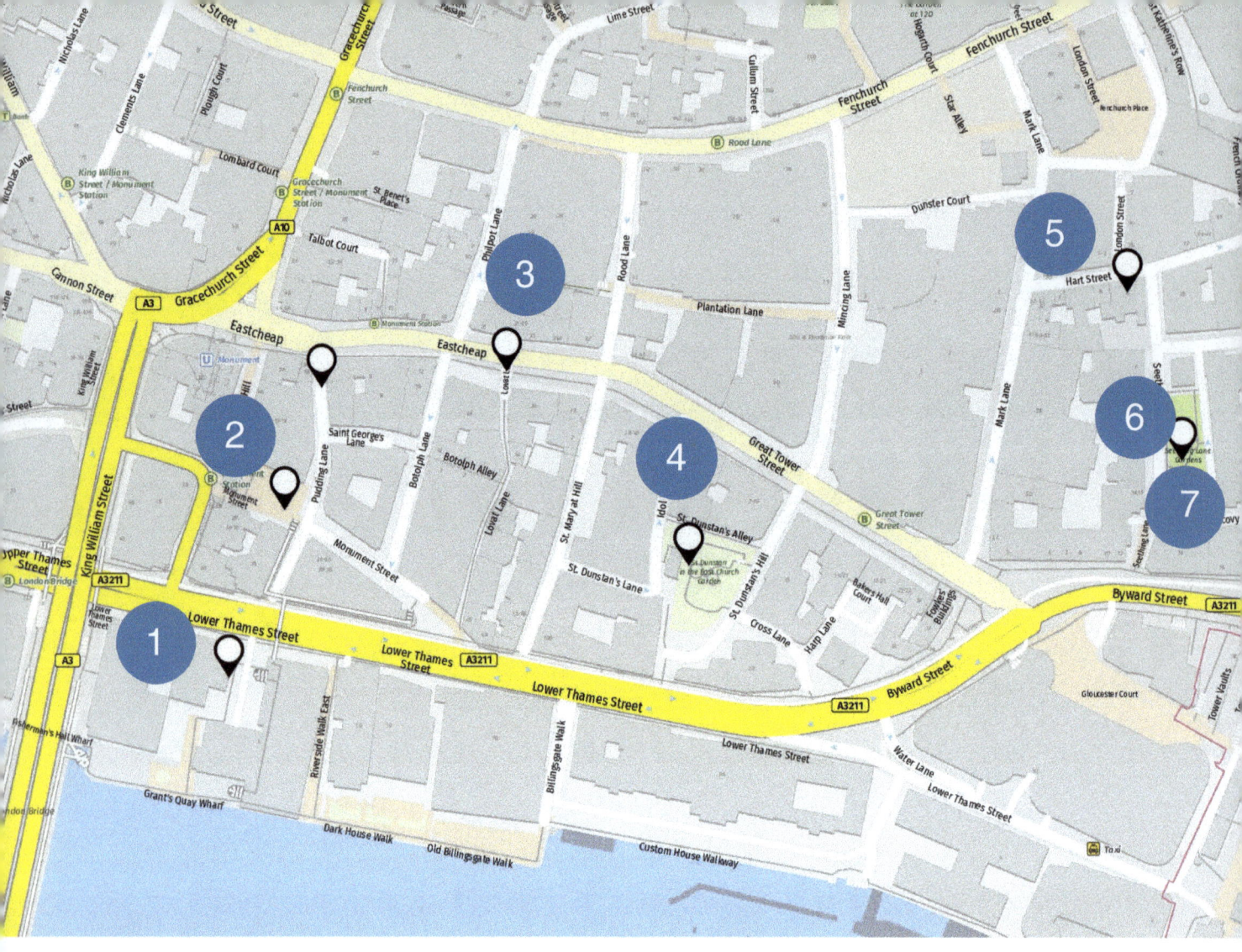

Stop 1: The Monument

Stop 2: Pudding Lane

Stop 3: St Magnus the Marytn

Stop 4: Lovat Lane

Stop 5: St Dunstans-in-the East

Stop 6: St Olaves Hart Street

Stop 7: Seething Lane Garden

Stop 1 - The Monument

On the 2nd of September 1666, a fire broke out here in the bakery of Thomas Farriner. It then spread across London destroying around 80% of the city. The monument was designed by Robert Hooke who originally designed it as a telescope but it didn't work because of the vibrations from traffic on the road. There are 311 steps to the top. There is a stone relief on one side showing King Charles II who was the king at the time.

Directions: Turn around and cross the space towards the plaque.

The Monument

Stop 2 - Pudding Lane

It was early on Sunday morning when Fire broke out. The Mayor came and looked and thought it wasn't a big problem and wouldn't pull his friends houses down as a fire break. At the time many people were quick to find someone to blame for the fire. They accused the French and the Dutch who England was at war with. They also blamed the Catholics as there was a lot of persecution against Catholics at the time.

Directions: Walk down Pudding Lane cross Lower Thames Street at the crossing.

Pudding Lane

St Magnus the Marytr

Stop 3 - St Magnus the Marytr
This was one of the first churches destroyed by the Fire. Look inside at the old fire engine and the model of old London Bridge inside. The church used to be at the start of the old London Bridge before the new bridge was moved up the river. There is a clock from 1707 on the outside of the church.

Directions: Re-cross the crossing on Lower Thames Street and walk along the street and up Lovat Lane.

Stop 4 - Lovat Lane
This is one of the old narrow streets of London. You can see the old cobbled street with a middle gutter section for water and waste to run down into the river at the bottom of the lane. Can you find the entrance to the church St Mary-at-Hill? Can you find a marking in the wall? This was used by the people building the church after the fire. This church was also badly damaged in another more recent fire in 1988.

Directions: Walk up the lane and turn right on Eastcheap. Turn right down Idol lane until you reach the church.

Lovat Lane

The Great Fire of London - 1666

Stop 5 - St Dunstans-in-the East

This church was damaged but survived the Fire. The architect Sir Christopher Wren designed a new tower. He built 51 churches in the city of London after the fire. At that time many more people lived in that part of London so they needed lots of churches for everyone. This church was bombed in the second world war so it was decided to leave it as a garden as you see it today. Each of Wren's churches is a different design and many are open in the week so go and have a look.

Directions: Walk up St Dunstan's Hill and cross the road on Great Tower Street. Turn left on Byward Street then left on Marks Lane. Turn into the churchyard.

St Dunstans-in-the East

Stop 6 - St Olaves Hart Street

We know so much about the Great Fire of London thanks to Samuel Pepys, who wrote a detailed diary about it. This was the church he attended. He lived opposite and used to have a covered entrance to the church from his house across the road. Can you see the old doorway on the wall of the church? In 1665, the year before the fire, there was a Great Plague where around 100,000 people died in London. The level of the graveyard is so high because there were so many extra bodies to bury.

Directions: Walk across the road down to Seething Lane Garden.

St Olaves Hart Street

Seething Lane Garden

Stop 7 - Seething Lane Garden Seething Lane is the site of his former house. Pepys wrote in code so people couldn't understand his diary so he was very honest! He also had a pet monkey and played several musical instruments. He even buried his cheese and wine to protect it from the fire. Although much of the city was destroyed. London rose from the flames and was quickly rebuilt in stone.

The Great Fire of London - 1666

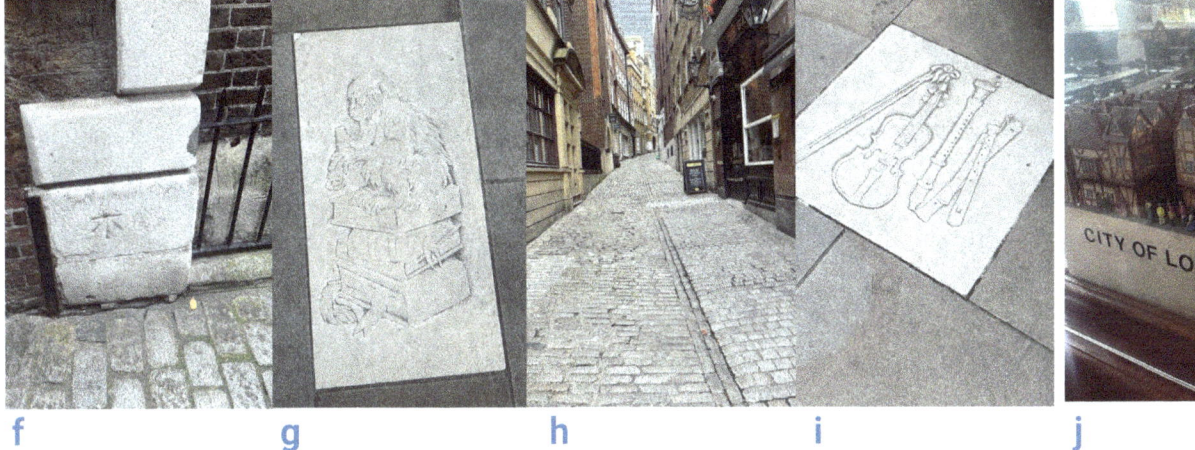

Find these details on the walk.
Match the word to the picture

1. Carved relief   Answer [ ]
2. Old fire engine   Answer [ ]
3. Old London Bridge   Answer [ ]
4. Tower   Answer [ ]
5. Cobbles   Answer [ ]
6. Builders marking   Answer [ ]
7. Gutter   Answer [ ]
8. Monkey   Answer [ ]
9. Musical Instruments   Answer [ ]
10. Graveyard   Answer [ ]

Match the following words to describe Samuel Pepys

1. Wig

2. Diary

3. Quill

4. Pocket

5. Cuff

What have you learned about the Great Fire of London?

_____

_____

_____

_____

The Great Fire of London - 1666

Notes

Answers:
Roman London, page 10: 1.g 2.c 3.a 4.f 5.d 6.h 7.i 8.j 9.b 10.e
Medieval London 500-1500 CE, page 18: 1.g 2.d 3.a 4.f 5.c 6.i 7.e 8.h 9.j 10.b
Legal London, page 26: 1.i 2.e 3.b 4.g 5.f 6.h 7.j 8.d 9.a 10.c
Women in London, page 34: 1.e 2.f 3.d 4.h 5.i 6.g 7.j 8.a 9.b 10.c
The Great Fire of London, page 42: 1.b 2.d 3.j 4.e 5.h 6.f 7.a 8.g 9.i 10.c

www.ingramcontent.com/pod-product-compliance
Lightning Source LLC
Chambersburg PA
CBHW040044090426
42734CB00024B/3491